My Favorite Book

A Book of Poems

Poems by
Nikki Grimes

Art by
Vaccaro and Associates

This edition published in 1990 by Gallery Books, an imprint of W.H. Smith Publishers, Inc., 112 Madison Avenue, New York, NY 10016.
Produced by Twin Books, 15 Sherwood Place, Greenwich, CT 06830
ISBN 0-8317-2349-1   Printed in Spain

Twin Books

GALLERY BOOKS

My Favorite Book

I like to read once in a while,
like morning, noon and night.
I like to read most any book
that I can find in sight.

I love a good, long mystery,
with secrets on each page.
I love a book about a zoo,
with lions in a cage.

I love to read about the past,
when dinosaurs were here,
or read of places far away.
(Books make them seem so near!)

I love adventure stories, where
the hero saves the day,
or tales about seafaring men
on ships that sail away.

I like a dragon story, with
a damsel in distress,
or stories about cowboys in
the wild and wacky west.

I like a book of poetry
most any place or time.
I love to read the rhythm, and
it's fun to learn the rhyme.

I guess I love most any kind
of book that you can name.
Sometimes I'd rather read a book
than play the greatest game.

I love to read once in a while,
like morning, noon and night.
I love to read most any book
that I can find in sight!

Secrets

A secret is a thing you share
with someone special, who will care
about the way you feel inside,
when there's a hurt you want to hide.

Or else a secret thing might be
a joke, or game, or star you see
some starry night when just you two
stare from a window at the view.

Sometimes a secret is a song—
you sing a verse, I sing along.
You've got a secret now? That's fine!
You tell me yours, I'll tell you mine!

Dots

Dots are great!
They're more than spots.
There's nothing quite like polka dots.

I mean, there's nothing to compare,
unless it's hearts—now those are rare!
The tiny ones are neat, you know,
on dresses, shoes, or on a bow.

Now, bows are wonderful to wear
on belts, on skirts, or in your hair.
But once again, I've got to say
that polka dots just make my day!

All Alone

No one's at home.
I'm all alone.
I stare and stare at the telephone.

I wait and wait,
and wait some more,
but no one calls. It's such a bore!

I clean the house,
I bake, I sew—
there's nothing left to do, you know.

And then I think:
I'll call my friend!
My pal! My buddy to the end!

I grab the phone,
no longer blue.
I smile, and laugh, and talk with you!

Seaside

In summertime, I see the sea.
The sun is warm; it smiles at me.
I dream I'm princess of the land.
I build tall castles in the sand.
I pick up shells along the shore.
I find sand dollars, rocks, and more.
(There's nothing like the sea!)

I ride the waves and splash around.
I listen to the whistling sound
you sometimes hear inside a shell.
(I love the sea, as you can tell.)
In summertime, I see the sea.
The sun is warm; it smiles at me.
(There's nothing like the sea!)

A Dream Come True

There were not always planes and trains
or lights and kites, or cellophane,
until somebody had a dream
and made that dream come true.

Before there was a music box,
or telephones or cuckoo clocks,
there was somebody with a dream
who made that dream come true.

Before we flew to outer space,
made wheels, or cars, or frilly lace,
there was somebody with a dream
who made that dream come true.

A dream is something fresh and new.
Work hard at it, and see it through.
Today, begin to dream a dream,
then make that dream come true!

The Fib

I told a fib, a little one,
an eeny, weeny, teeny one.
I planted it in someone's mind.
He watered it, and then, with time,
the fib grew like a big oak tree.
My gosh! Did that fib come from me?

I told a fib, a little one,
an eeny, weeny, teeny one.
It towered over sea and land—
that little fib got out of hand.
Too late to try and fix it now.
Besides, I don't think I know how!

I told a fib, a little one,
an eeny, weeny, teeny one.
But fibs are dangerous, I found,
for they can grow by leaps, by bounds.
I'll never tell a fib again!
I hope that you won't either, friend!

Summer Camp

I went to camp last summer,
and I took my ball and bat.
I took along some bug spray,
a sleeping bag and hat.

The first day we went hiking.
Then we rowed across the lake.
Later I peeled potatoes
for someone else to bake.

At lunch we ate a little,
and then we washed a lot.
There were a zillion dishes.
(I only saw one pot.)

Then later came the baskets
they forced us all to weave.
I was so bored and tired,
I told them I would leave!

That night we had our dinner—
some kind of hash, I think.
And then, of course—you guessed it—
they marched us to the sink!

The day was almost over.
I dreamt about my bed.
But first there were the camp songs
they made us sing, instead!

We sat around the fire.
The night was getting cool.
I said (but no one heard me),
"I'd rather be in school!"

I've never been so tired!
I begged them on my knee,
"Oh, please let me go home now!
This camp is killing me!"

The next day was much better.
The hiking was okay.
My basket turned out pretty.
I still have it today!

The days passed by so quickly!
I made a special friend.
We rowed our boat all over.
Why did camp have to end?

It wasn't long before I
was back in school once more.
I sang camp songs all winter,
until my throat was sore.

I'm going back to camp now,
and I can hardly wait!
I still hate washing dishes,
but summer camp is great!

Dress-Up

My favorite game is dress-up.
I play it all the time.
I love to try on different clothes
and make believe that I'm...
a movie star or princess,
a bride or tennis pro.
When you dress up, you can pretend
you're anything, you know!

I try on hats and glasses,
I try on scarves and shirts.
I try on big and little bows,
and silly, frilly skirts.
Then, when my playtime's over,
I put my clothes away.
I go back to just being me—
until some other day!

My Diary

I have a diary that's red.
I hide it underneath my bed.
I keep it for my very own.
I write in it when I'm alone.

I write about the things I do,
like going to the park or zoo.
I write about the things I see,
about my friends, what I shall be.

Sometimes I write about my dreams,
and they become more real, it seems.
I write about what makes me sad,
and somehow it's not quite so bad.

I use my diary every night,
and then, when I turn off the light,
I take my diary that's red
and hide it underneath my bed.

Spring

The flower buds say spring is here.
The clouds are thick. The rain is near.
The air smells clean. The grass does, too.
I love the spring, when things are new!

Summer

The summer sun burns through my clothes.
I make my way down to the beach.
I squish the sand between my toes,
and nibble on a sweet, cold peach.

Fall

I gathered up some leaves last fall,
and pressed them in my favorite book.
I liked the gold ones best of all.
I hope you'll come and take a look!

Winter

Some winter days are cold and clear.
Sometimes the snow comes up to here.
I wear my mittens, coat and hat,
build snowmen that are round and fat!

Ballerina

When I grow up,
I think I'll be
a ballerina. Wait and see!

I'll wear a crown.
I'll dress in lace.
I'll dance tiptoe from place to place.

I'll spin and twirl.
I'll leap so high
I'll very nearly touch the sky!

When I grow up,
I think I'll be
a ballerina. Wait and see!

My Doll

Sometimes my doll sits on my lap,
closes her eyes, and takes a nap.
Sometimes she crawls, or laughs or talks.
Sometimes I take my doll for walks.
There are lots of things that she can do,
but sometimes, I need you.

I often comb her hair and try
to brush it, hoping she won't cry.
But when she does, I hug her. Then
she laughs and smiles at me again.
There are lots of things my doll can do,
but often, I need you.

I always rock my doll to sleep,
then lay her down without a peep.
But first I hold her very tight,
and wait until she squeaks, "Good night!"
There are lots of things that she can do,
but always, I need you.

With you I share big things, it seems,
like scary thoughts and special dreams.
Sometimes my doll seems almost real,
but she can't think, or dream or feel.
There are lots of things my doll can do,
but she can't love like you.

Snow Fantasy

I'd love to take
a big snowflake
and sew it on my sweater.
(Two snowflakes would be better!)

Or I could string
a row of them—
they'd make a lovely belt.
(But then, of course, they'd melt!)

I'd like to pour
a cup or more
of snowflakes in a jar.
(It hasn't worked, so far!)

I know, I know—
I can't keep snow.
But make-believe is fun.
(So don't tell anyone!)

Imagination

When I'm all grown and fancy-free,
there are many things I want to be.
And I can be them all! You see?
Imagination is the key!

I look inside where visions grow.
I'm Mother Nature, don't you know;
an astronaut...a doctor—me!
Imagination is the key!

I'm sitting on the high trapeze.
I'm a reporter, if you please;
a tennis pro...a pilot—gee!
Imagination is the key!

I play piano; I play ball.
I can be anything at all.
And you can, too—just wait and see.
Imagination is the key!

Rainy Day

The rain is pouring down outside.
The sky is gray, and storm clouds hide
the smiling sun.

There's nothing much to do today.
It's much too wet outside to play
or skip or run.

I call my friends, but they're all out,
so I decide to write about
the raging storm.

I write a rhyme or two for fun,
and by the time the poem's done,
I'm feeling warm.

I'm glad I had this rainy day.
I did some things I always say
I want to do.

I won't mind if it rains tonight.
Tomorrow will be warm and bright,
and smell like new!

Chocolate Dreams

Last night I had a chocolate dream.
(I know you'll think it's funny.)
I dreamt about a forest where
I met a chocolate bunny.

The chocolate bunny led me to
a field of chocolate roses.
He showed me hills of chocolate fudge.
(The smell tickled our noses.)

Later we swam a chocolate lake,
and climbed a chocolate mountain.
We raced to Chocolate Park, and then
drank from a chocolate fountain.

I stuffed myself with chocolate fudge,
and ice cream topped with cherries.
I ate from chocolate apple trees,
and gobbled chocolate berries.

When I was through, I felt so ill!
I woke up in a hurry.
I hope the bunny I meet next
is warm, and soft, and furry!

School Days

I wish we could skip the first week of school.
I wish we could start the week after.
The first week is scary, lonely and new.
The next week is crammed full of laughter!

It's hard to fit in and make a new friend.
(Why is it that everyone's taller?)
But once you have made a new pal or two,
your classmates seem suddenly smaller!

I know we can't skip the first week of school.
I know we can't start the week after.
So let's try and rush that first week on through,
so next week will get here much faster!

My Purse

I love my purse, my very own!
I keep my treasures in it.
My comb is there for dolly's hair.
She'll need it any minute!

My purse is fat with money, too,
five nickels and one quarter.
My purse has lots of pockets that
help keep these things in order.

I love my purse; it's just my size!
It fits right on my shoulder.
I'll keep my purse till I am grown,
and use it when I'm older!

A Three Party

One person can read,
or paint, or draw.
Two can play checkers,
or ride a seesaw.
But what in the world
can you do with three?
Why, just bring out
the cookies and tea!

Colors

The other day I thought I'd try
to find a new dress I could buy.
I told the salesgirl I liked red.
She brought out burgundy, instead,
and berry, crimson—scarlet, too.
Then came vermillion. I was through!
I left that store and said good-bye.
I knew another store to try.

I asked the salesman there for blue.
"Fine!" said he. "Will indigo do?
There's cobalt, turquoise, cerulean, or...
is slate the blue you're looking for?"
"I thought I knew," I told the man.
I left the store. I almost ran!
I thought, "Next time, I'll ask for green.
I'm sure they'll know just what I mean."

But I was wrong, I learned in time.
They brought out olive, forest, lime,
kelly and khaki, mint and bice!
The salesgirls offered their advice.
"Tell me," said one, "have you tried red?"
I screamed, put on my clothes, and fled!
I calmed myself so I could think:
"Perhaps the shade I need is pink.

"Pink is the best color to choose.
There aren't as many pinks as blues."
But I was wrong, as you might guess.
I wondered, "Do I *need* a dress?"
I looked at pinks till I turned blue—
magenta, fuchsia, cerise, too.
I thought I knew my colors, but
I'm not sure now just what is what!

That day, I saw purples galore—
soft lilac, lavender, and more!
I saw canary yellow; sand,
umber, sienna, ochre, and
caramel; peach and tangerine;
china blue, ultramarine...
Why, there are colors by the ton!
(I'm sure that I saw every one!)

I guess I learned a thing or two:
Red isn't red, blue isn't blue.
That is to say, colors are made
in lights and darks of every shade.
One day, I'll learn each shade by name.
Till then, I'll call all reds the same.
But next time I go to a store,
I'll know just what I'm looking for!

Quarrel

My friend and I, we had a fight,
'cause she was wrong, and I was right.
Of course, she said that I was wrong,
but I refused to play along.
She yelled at me, and I yelled, too.
I thought, "Well, then, our friendship's through!"

Then just before I turned to go,
it hit me that I didn't know
exactly what had made us fight.
Just who was wrong, and who was right?
What did it matter, in the end?
I didn't want to lose my friend!

I told my friend that I was sad
that I had yelled and gotten mad.
"All right," she said, "I'm sorry, too.
I know I shouldn't yell at you.
Besides, you are my best friend yet.
So let's forgive, and let's forget!"

Jump~Rope Rhyme

Minnie is my first name,
Mouse is my last.
I can tie a bow
while the rope turns fast.

I don't need a dollar,
I don't need a dime.
But I can use a Penny
most any old time.

Penny's on my left side,
Daisy's on my right,
So I can jump rope
from morning till night!

Pets

I'd like to have a puppy.
I'd like to have a cat.
But when it comes to bathing them,
I don't think I'd like that!

Now kitties are so quiet!
They wear pads on their paws.
But I don't think I'd like it
when I had to cut their claws!

A puppy is so clever!
It barks back when I talk.
But I don't want to be the one
to take it for a walk!

Someday I'll have a puppy.
Someday I'll have a cat.
For now, I'll keep my favorite doll.
I'm certain about that!

Slumber Party

My party was the best one yet!
My friends came by and spent the night.
We had a crazy pillow fight.
We laughed until we cried.

My party was the best one yet!
We ate popcorn and watched TV.
We played dress-up and sang off-key.
We danced. At least, we tried!

My party was the best one yet!
We whispered secrets all night through.
We listened to some records, too.
We played two games, or three.

My party was the best one yet!
And you know why it was such fun?
My friends! Yes, each and every one
was there along with me!